M000190904

S.H.I.F.T.!

Keeping your Focus to Maximize your Potential.

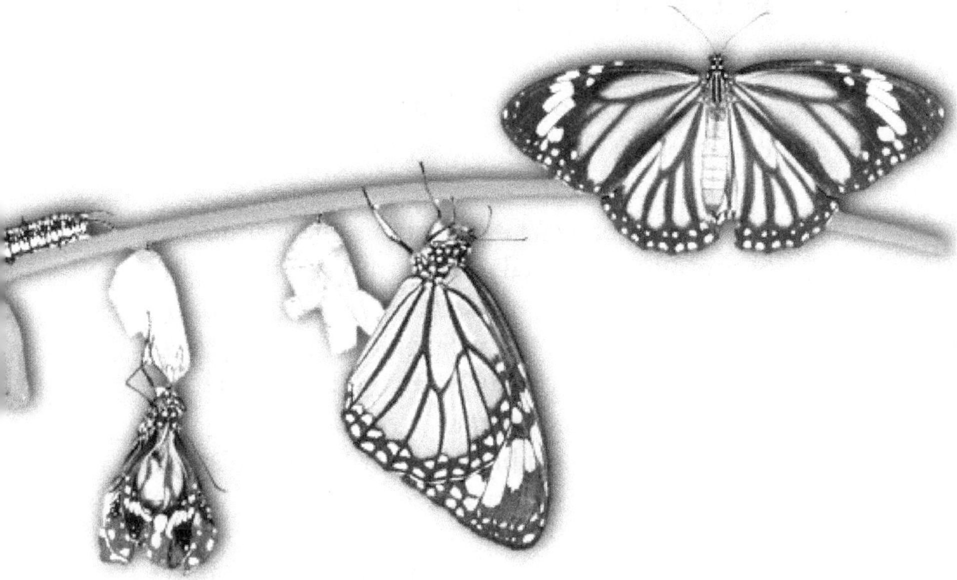

CLARINDRIA ADDISON

SHIFT Consulting LLC

Published by Shift Consulting LLC

Library of Congress Control Number: 2021918917
ISBN 978-0-578-99176-4
Printed in the United States of America

Dedication

To my three where do I begin? Please forgive me as I've said before I did the best I could with what I knew at that time. What I know now, I am sharing with you and the world. You all have seen me up working sleepless nights, crying, meditating and you must know that every single thing that I've done has been so that I could encourage you to be better than me.

Caitlyn my first born when I named you I said her name is going to be Caitlyn Monae' because she'll be famous one day your spirit is so kind you have a way with people that will get you in many rooms...my nurse daughter proud mama.

My Jacob people probably wonder why I say "my Jacob". I will share with those who don't know Jacob was my gift from God via my sister. He is where I learned unconditional love because no matter what I committed to love you like you were mines and I hope I have done so.

Dedication

TJ my stuff doer you are mine and your daddy's child you have all of the strengths of both of us put together...resilient independent tenacious intelligent and kind. Continue your journey and commit to loving yourself and know that you get what you put in and the world is at your feet.

My brother Donell, he doesn't like that name lol. Know that you inspired me to be great. I saw you working two jobs and having all that you desired.

My sister Na, you made sure I knew how to spell my name and read before I got to school. You do not play about your "baby " sister to this day.

To everyone that I could not name individually know that I learned a lesson from each and everyone of you that in some way shape or form made me better.

Table of Content

Foreword

I want to say that this is a love offering in the form of a love-centered book. May we all be blessed by Clarindria's lived and learned experiences. May we accept this offering for its highest purpose and choose to S.H.I.F.T. together. Strength is found within intentional planning and that is exactly what these pages offer us. A way to process opportunity that grows all that is possible for each of us. Tap into your gifts, grow in community, let love and opportunity in as the time is always now. To my dear friend who offers us a glimpse of her soul in an effort to catapult our process of self-actualization through the power of S.H.I.F.T., I say thank you. May all you give in the name of progress and endless possibilities rise to meet you daily.

JoAnne Johnson Sabir

JoAnne Johnson Sabir
Entrepreneur/Developer

PART ONE

The Situation

"You should never view your challenges as a disadvantage. Instead, it's important for you to understand that your experience facing and overcoming adversity is actually one of your biggest advantages."

~Michelle Obama

CHAPTER ONE

Same S.H.I.F.T., Different Toilet

The Awakening

Have you ever been in a coma? I was in a self-induced coma for almost twenty years. I was awake, but unconscious. I was alive, but my brain was functioning at its lowest stage of alertness. I could not shake it; it was as if I was sleepwalking. There were a series of unfortunate events that took me down this road that I had no idea how I would recover. I got into the habit of moving forward with no thought of how to deal with the trauma I had faced. All the things a person typically has going on in their life has happened to me: survivor of rape, domestic violence, viewing my mother's death... but I had a choice to make. My decision was not to be the victim. I had to figure out how to get through this situation without all the pieces available. There was no manual to follow and for me, I was, 'The First' in my family to...well, you fill in the blank. I was blazing a trail and was supported by people who saw the potential in me, but they lacked the tools and direction to help me.

I grew up in the inner city during a time where role models were few and far between. It was the '80s and I modeled success from the families on television and the few people in my neighborhood who had beat the odds to live a middle-class lifestyle. That lifestyle was not a reality for me; we were poor and suffered from the same scenarios that plagued those in similar socioeconomic situations. Growing up Black in the '80s meant it was impossible to not be affected by the crack era in some way. My family was hit head-on with a force that derailed all hopes of any dreams being realized. It was like the lights were turned off and a dark shadow hovered over our community. My four siblings were addicted to drugs and or alcohol. I was the baby of the family but had the most responsibility. Mom always had multiple jobs, which did not leave much time for us, but she had no choice. We received government assistance for a short time; it was just enough to keep the lights on. I remember coming home with my mother once and the lights were turned off. She went to flick the switch, and nothing happened. I ran around the house and checked to see if the toilet would still flush and the water would come on. I was six and had no idea what had happened. I had no clue the power had been turned off. My childlike innocence was in full bloom. Seeing my siblings struggle is where I began to exercise resilience. Whatever the cost, I did not want to be an addict. They warned me of the dangers of drugs, even though they succumbed to the trap that ensnared so many. I was just protected from the dangers many were exposed to. Those same elements destroyed families and communities we called home from the ghettos in California to my block in Milwaukee, Wisconsin.

Hard to see past what's in front of you. Most people are not able to see the forest for the trees, but I was. I knew there was more to life than what I was seeing, but I had no idea how to get to it. I was the first in my family to go to college. Although everyone had jobs, no one had 'a career'. I could see the big picture when many where I lived could not. Without vision, it became impossible to set goals and work towards them. Many Black women felt they had no one to talk with who was knowledgeable, listened to their challenges, kept it real, and gave feedback without judgment. While finding genuine support can seem like finding a needle in a haystack, what makes it even more challenging is that many live by a 'no new friends' motto, which leaves them operating in a silo: alone to solve problems they do not have the answers to nor the agency to figure them out.

I am blessed. Many people see my success and perceive me as one who will listen and help them get unstuck. But, for many years I feared people judging me. It was the culmination of different experiences and jealous people pretending to be happy for me. But I had to move forward. I knew what I did not want. I was around drugs and poverty. I knew I did not want that. I focused on the goal and continued doing what I knew was right.

Acknowledging trauma.

We have all experienced traumatic events, it may not always be a major accident. It could be divorce, loss of relationships, or even your upbringing. When you talk about trauma or loss, you have to go through all the stages of grief to get through it. We often do not allow ourselves this time or even acknowledge that we have experienced trauma. My siblings, being older than me, wanted to ensure I didn't make the same mistakes they made. Until I was in the fifth grade, they would always say things like, "You're smart, you can do it!" or "Keep going!" My success was celebrated until crack moved in and addiction took over. That was when I had to find new motivation and encourage myself. My encouragement for not becoming what I was seeing daily was real. Over a few years, everyone lost themselves to crack. Everyone experiences trauma. Then we fight through the trauma to achieve success. Things not going as we planned them can be a part of the cycle of grief and trauma. So, when you go through something traumatic you must have the coping skills necessary to overcome that challenge. Without these skills, doubt comes into play and hinders progress. Most are afraid of the unknown, the process, failure, and even fear itself. This trauma was often the cause of me getting stuck in my emotions and allowing them to overpower my thought process. I went from sad, to mad, angry, and then frustrated. I was stuck here and could not get past it.

All talk, no action.

I have an associate I've known for many years. Several years ago, he got the idea to start a business. I was excited for him and I believed he would be great at it. I also knew he was stressed and burnt out at his job, he was beginning to hate it, and it was making him sick. Although he made great money, he was not happy. I bought him T.D. Jakes' book, Soar.

I was sure it would help him gain perspective. I love gifting books because sometimes it may be the spark someone needs to push through. Before I gave him the book I wrote a message for him that simply read: Know that you are great, you're powerful beyond measure and you have so many talents that you can use but you have to make a plan for yourself and do it. I think this book will help you get started. After that, he launched his business and it appeared that he was making progress. He told me he was encouraged when he read the book. He realized he was capable, but the problem was he could not get out of his own way. At the time, he was caring for his nephew, had mounting bills, and was on a leave of absence. Having all things going on that had become distractions to block his blessings and keep him mentally stuck. It had become easy to make excuses and procrastinate rather than do the work to change his circumstances and ultimately his life.

He continued to have false starts and the business never really got off the ground. He used his job as an excuse to not pursue that big picture. He was consumed with the immediate, like so many of us, that he was missing the process of attaining his goal. He had so much God-given talent that he was not focusing on, therefore was missing his purpose. I explained if he focused on his gifts he would be blessed tenfold. The travesty is that he could not see it. He had never had people encourage him or tell him he did well. So in his forty-something years of life, he sought approval, rather than approving himself and believing he was enough. You cannot wait for someone else to give it to you, you have to prove yourself worthy by going to get it if it is something you want. So if you're waiting for somebody to tell you that you're doing a great job, just STOP WAITING! You are going through the motions. The hamster wheel is more like a stagnation circle because you're not willing to step off and take on the obstacles that stand in the way of your success. I had to separate myself from that energy. I cannot want it more than you do. So, if you're not going to use some of this information and take the steps to improve your situation, STOP READING NOW!

Failing the test, repeating the lesson.

In all fairness, life is a test, we just do not know the right answers to the test or have access to the people to ask for help. We have been taught to wear the mask because we're scared to be seen or rather judged for our ignorance. We would rather look like we have it all together when we do not. Sometimes we need someone to say, "Ok, this is what we are doing now, and this is how we move forward." But this rarely happens, so we must find a way to get what we need to progress in life. Doing nothing keeps you in the same place that you've been, experiencing the same outcomes. Change means doing something different.

If the goal is to do something different, then that is exactly what you must do. It's about discovering yourself and what makes you tick. I'm just a facilitator whose goal is to help you get to where you desire to be, but you must want it.

You must be willing to put in the work to get it and go through the process. It is not easy, but it IS worth it. Most are going through the same motions, but they do not know the pathway and they are not asking the right questions. The fact is there are no stupid questions. The great Tupac Shakur said, "Even a genius asks a question." So why don't we? When we try to figure things out alone, we often fail. Not knowing doesn't mean you're stupid, but not asking for directions could mean just that. IJS

You may have a college degree and have raised multiple kids, but for some things, you need a road map to help get you to where you want to be. I remember Oprah saying, "When we know better, we do better." That stuck because I believed it. So, my role is to make sure you are conscious and equipped with the tools you need and be motivated to apply the techniques I share to help facilitate your win.

Crabs in the barrel mentality.

Many people don't feel like they are enough, due to the lack of support. For Black women, seeing somebody else do well can be hard, mainly because it may appear as if there are only so many slots for "us" as Black women. It's a struggle that a mindset fueled with jealousy often prevails. If you are not surrounded by supportive people, life will be more challenging. You need cheerleaders or people in the background encouraging you to succeed. It's even more challenging for Black women because we encourage each other even less. Shouldn't we be happy for each other? But we often suffer from the crabs in a barrel mentality, which is a way of thinking best described by the saying, "if I can't have it, you can't either". While one crab could easily escape, its efforts will be undermined by the other crabs, ensuring the group's collective demise. This mentality has kept many Black people stuck, stagnant, or in a rut, waiting for someone to save them.

During my early years of entrepreneurship, I often didn't tell people what I was doing, until

I was deep into it. I did not want to deal with the same questions from the naysayers or the "Debbie Downers" who hang on to negativity and make you feel like whatever you want to accomplish is impossible. Our environments often are not conducive to our success. Let me say that again, our environments are often not conducive to our success. You must surround yourself with people who are genuinely happy, encouraging, and want to see you win. You need to hear from someone who is where you are trying to go.

Black women living below their potential is a travesty. We have all these women out of position and roaming the earth when they are supposed to be walking in their purpose, which someone somewhere is waiting on them to do, so they can then realize theirs. We are all connected and are more powerful together rather than apart or divided. It is culture-based as our experiences are very different. We have been programmed. It has been ingrained in us to think and behave this way, but the cycle can be broken.

Playing our part in the problem.

A few years ago, I moved my office into a new building that was a project located not too far from the street I grew up on. The building is called Sherman Phoenix; it was opened in 2018 after a racial uprising left a bank building vacant. One of the developers, who would later become a friend, and her business partner decided to restore and redevelop the building to house 27 small businesses; 25 were owned by people of color. Most of the business owners who opened their businesses were selling products. I knew I wasn't selling anything, but I felt I needed to be there. It was significant for me because it was in my community, and I wanted to do whatever I could to make sure that the businesses who decided to call this new building home had what they needed to succeed. I did not then, nor do I now, have all the answers, but I have learned some things over my 20 years of experience, which includes running a program with a multi-million dollar budget. The experiences I had and the lessons I learned in business may be valuable to someone just starting. From bookkeeping tools and techniques to payroll systems to policy. It wasn't about what I could get, but rather what I could give. I had a couch in my office and other tenants would come and sit on my couch and share feelings of being overwhelmed or just help with the process. I was that person for many people. That's why I knew I needed to be involved in that project. I was not selling anything, but I had experiences and knowledge to offer to new entrepreneurs and whoever else was open to receiving it.

I'm a therapist, who out of necessity, became an entrepreneur. I use my clinical study to help with real-world practical business problems daily. What I have learned is the way we have been socialized as black people, but more specifically Black women plays a huge role in our current psyche. I recently asked my coaching clients what they needed help with, and the response went even deeper than I could have imagined. The women all provided a laundry list of areas where they needed support. One client gave me a list of 40 things she felt she needed to address to move her life forward. Now, the reality is that we're never going to be able to address that number of things in a short time; it's just not going to happen. This became a trend among the women. Of the four women I focused on, one had been homeless and three of them had master's degrees. The irony of the needs list my client provided was that she acknowledged it as being too much. Her response was, "I always do that". That statement was an admission of guilt to the syndrome known as "insanity" doing something we know does not work repeatedly but looking for a different outcome. That was holding her back. In my experience, I've found that this is a fallacy practiced by many. If you pick up that paper and look at the list, you're going to get overwhelmed and most likely you'll do nothing.

This was eye-opening and showed me that no one is immune. Although we are all different and come from different places, we all have common threads, which make us similar. Whether it's the challenges we face as Black

Women in America or the lack of support and guidance we've received from each other on our journey; the fact is we all need help. Nothing great accomplished was done alone. We each have had different struggles: fear of not making it out, no direction or reliable mentorship opportunities, or a poverty mentality that tells you what you cannot accomplish. Most of us have pulled through some of our toughest times and are still standing, which means, it IS possible to move past these challenges even though it doesn't seem like it. When it comes to "business" and deciding how we move forward with the ideas we have about our lives, we usually do not ask ourselves important questions like: Are you ready to overcome fears, past mistakes, and other setbacks you've experienced to succeed? If you said yes, get ready to move past this moment to experience the life you envision. Don't get it twisted; it is not going to be easy, but I can promise you it will be worth it.

"Don't wait for permission, figure out what you need to be the heroine in your own story." ~Ava DuVernay

S.H.I.F.T. TIP:
Stop waiting for a perfect time to fly. There's no better time than now.

SHIFT NOTES

"When life gives you lemons, don't make lemonade; make pink lemonade, be unique."

~Wanda Sykes

CHAPTER TWO

Good S.H.I.F.T.! **Life CAN Be Good!**

Can you imagine a life filled with accomplished goals and all the success you ever envisioned? It may be difficult at first, but I am here to tell you it is possible. I remember feeling like I had not taken a breath in years. I had been on 'GO' mode. In that time, I started a new business which brought with it more responsibility, more commitment, and more time. I had been overcoming obstacles but by default. I was moving through my days on autopilot.

The trauma that I experienced put me in a coma. The tricky part is that I did not even realize I was in a coma. I could not see it until I started my self-healing. These experiences ushered in the awakening process that would change my world forever. I realized if it was not for the nonstop demands and the pressure, this solution would not have been birthed and I would not have had a path to follow or share. The process is important because life is a cycle and things tend to happen repeatedly. Your goal is to decide which position you will play. Will you be prepared for the next time it happens? Without a process, I can guarantee you will not. Without the process, I would not have been able to do any of the things that I have accomplished. I was raised in what most would consider the ghetto around people most considered to be forgotten. Poverty and drugs were a mainstay in my neighborhood, but I was able to see past the pain to create something that could help save me as well as the people I love. I pushed, applied myself, and overcame obstacles that could have killed me, but instead, they made me stronger. I earned a master's degree and I am recognized by the board of National Certified Counselors as a Licensed Professional Counselor and substance abuse counselor, which I chose for obvious reasons.

Life showed me what was important to me and I listened. I used my degree to help those who were vulnerable. I knew that feeling and wanted to help them avoid the dangers of doing nothing and hoping things changed.

Today, I own Hands at Home LLC, which has grown beyond what I could have ever envisioned. My agency provides services for adults with disabilities 24/7. I have grown the operation to three locations, and I currently employ 18 people including three of my family members. When my business began in 2016, one goal was to have three group homes in three years. I had three group homes in two years.

Realizing my vision not only changed the trajectory of my life, it also changed the lives of people I love. My oldest brother and sister both work for me. She is a supervisor and is nine years clean and he is eight years sober. I've also helped another sister launch two adult family homes. If you were sitting on a resource that could change the lives of the people you love, would you use it?

I did. And I had no idea taking those steps would have the impact it did in our lives.

Life personified.

I have been through a lot. I had to find my path and pursue it. Once I saw how it shifted my reality, I decided to share it. That solution gave me a pathway to follow that reduced my stress, provided clarity and structure to opportunities and life more abundantly. It increased my chances of success drastically. First, there's the value of the solution itself. I was the proof. What I learned was insightful. I had grown in knowledge, which gave me more power. The power was in the new confidence and level of achievement that I now had my sights set on. I was able to be comfortable in the decisions that I was making to move forward.

Being made aware of the benefits of getting out of my way served as the motivation to continue to seek answers and solutions. When we stop searching, we lose hope, become stagnant and stop growing. Knowing the benefit attracts you to the solution. Pursuing this pathway helped reduce my stress, concern, uncertainty, and a host of other challenges that were acting as proverbial weights on my back. The more I was able to shed, the closer I moved towards success. I became more and more effective in my actions as repeated success positioned me for more growth.

There are multiple ways to overcome the challenges you face. The key is you must begin, to have a chance to win. Finding a knowledgeable mentor is one way to overcome your challenges. Seek out someone who has already been where you're going and can provide guidance and insight along your journey. We all need someone to hold us accountable. You can also seek out ways to stay focused and set plans to achieve your goals. The challenge here is you will run into obstacles you will not yet know how to maneuver because you have never had the experience. The key is to seek help to identify the best option for your situation. This may take a few misses before you find a hit, but you cannot quit.

Benefits of the journey.

What I want to share with you will not only save you time but some pain and sleepless nights, too. I have shed the blood, sweat, and cried the tears that came with pitfalls and false starts. If you had the opportunity to travel a bumpy road full of potholes, dips, and debris versus a smoother path with directional signs to help you navigate, which one would you choose? If you decide to follow the process I outlined in this book, you will be one step closer to achieving your goals and reaching your desired destination. You'll gain a sense of accomplishment that's invaluable. You will move into a position to help others grow as you keep growing. Be reminded there is always room for growth and opportunities to plant seeds in others that support their learning and development.

When I implemented this in my life opportunities increased, I had more time for myself and my decision-making skills improved drastically. Stress was gone and I felt I was in control of my life. I was steering the boat and navigating uncharted waters. It is amazing the difference it makes when you have direction. Knowing what you need to succeed saves time and angst. This is essential in finding purpose, satisfaction, and joy in your life. Feeling focused made me feel more positive and in control of my life. By setting goals and having a plan you reduce the risk of uncertainties and wasteful activities. The key is to just start. The lessons are learned while you are acting. In action, your confidence is increased.

Tap into your power.

When I ignored a problem, I felt miserable. Hardships come with unexpected stressors and can bring feelings of disappointment. I know this from experience. It's not your problems that are creating your suffering, but your resistance to your challenges that cause your unhappiness. As you overcome your challenges, you will experience more joy in your life. You gain strength and confidence that you can overcome anything.

I recently took my annual trip to Jamaica, which I use to reflect and reposition myself for the year ahead. As I sat by the pool, sipping on a fruity cocktail with an umbrella positioned just so, I began to think about my children and how they are on the right track. One of my sons is in college, my daughter is a registered nurse, and my other son has begun his career in the Air Force. My business and my life are on the track I envisioned, headed for the destination I manifested. I work for myself, but the keyword is "work." Hard work and perseverance are huge components of my success. And you will find them to be key components of your success strategy as well.

My journey has been turbulent, and I would not change anything about it because it made me who I am today. I hope to help you navigate your journey and coach you to completion, mixing your journey with greater wisdom and harmony than I experienced.

My passion is in helping people get to the next phase of their lives. My goal is to provide a safe space to explore your thoughts, feelings, and concerns as it relates to your journey. Just like I did, equipped with the right recipe you can overcome the obstacles that threaten your potential success. Use this book as a resource to not only you, but the people that depend on you, to make S.H.I.F.T. happen.

S.H.I.F.T. TIP:

Find your motivation for pushing forward and use it for your fuel.

SHIFT NOTES

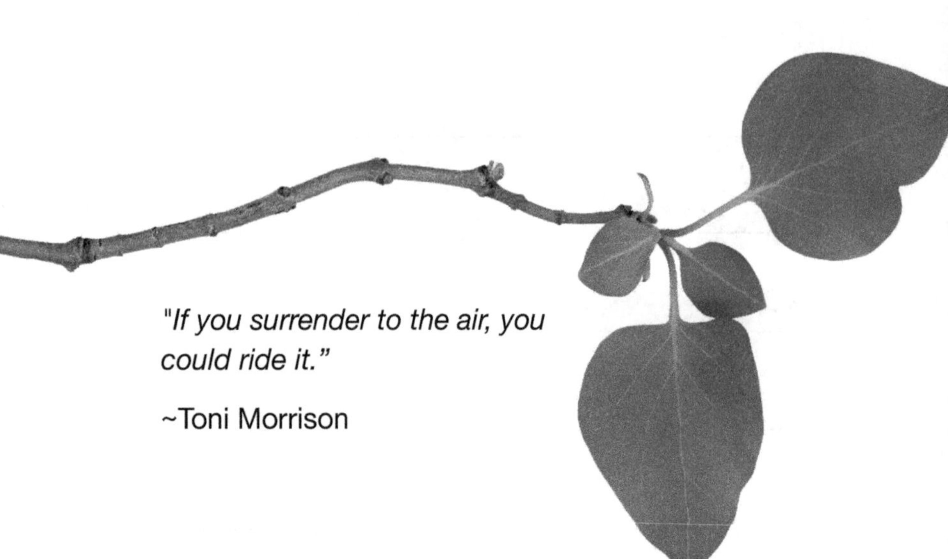

"If you surrender to the air, you could ride it."

~Toni Morrison

CHAPTER THREE

Starting S.H.I.F.T.
There's Always a Way to Do It.

There are thousands of stories about the person who had it all but lost it. There are also the stories of people with so much potential they never activate. The fact is it comes down to a decision. You decided to read this book to overcome the challenges of achieving your goals and realizing your dreams. We make decisions - or our decisions make us. Our decisions determine our outcomes. I decided to have a career that allows me to be available to, and for, my children. That decision allowed me to dictate the terms of how I earn my living and will affect my children for the rest of their lives. My 'being present' gave them the confidence they needed to position them for success. Growing up in an inner-city, in one of the worst zip codes in the country, I knew I wanted more than I saw. Growing up, my role models were from the Cosby Show and Family Ties. They gave me a frame of reference of what family should or maybe could look like. It attracted me, I wanted that life.

Get unstuck.

Women often get stuck without having a trusted person or resource that can help you figure out the answers to get your life back on track once derailed. These are steps you can do every day to get back on track. I often tell the women I coach that it is really about them holding themselves accountable. I'm just a voice in the background reminding you of your responsibility and cheering you on to what's possible. You must make a decision and say to yourself, "This is what I want! I know when I sit down and I write this list of things I have to do, the only way it is going to get done is if I do it!"

If you do nothing, you'll find yourself stuck in a circle waiting for something to happen. For the solution I'm sharing to work in your life, you must first apply it and then work the steps. Trial and error are the only way.

I don't think of the steps as being difficult, but it does come down to how bad you want to go to the next level. Sure, everyone says they want to level up but are they willing to do the work? Many people I meet are not. I had to ask myself the question that I now ask all my clients before we begin to work together. I have developed a sixth sense that reads through the BS. It's ok if you're not ready if you are moving towards being ready. I knew I was ready, so it was only a matter of engagement rather than merely talking about it. Maybe it's a New Orleans cultural thing: I was told we did not talk about what we were working on until it was complete. You must ask yourself if you are ready to experience the life you envisioned for yourself. I knew after answering that I had to pursue that change. I knew that things were going to be changing for me and that it was going to be a process. I began to slowly move out of my comfort zone because I knew there was nothing there that would move me closer to overcoming. For so long I chose to stand in the background. I knew I needed to overcome my shyness, but I felt like I was being judged constantly. I never wanted to have my business in the street because I'm a private person, so I learned to move in silence.

The game is mental.

I want to be able to continue the lifestyle that I have currently made for myself. Now I am on this sped-up timeline to get to a certain level before I retire using the process that has gotten me to this point of my journey. I am working very aggressively. Growth is ongoing. Always growing, never grown, it is just a part of the process. We go through things, learn from those experiences and take those lessons to the next level. Everyone has their journey. There are several components of this spiritual, mental, and physical journey. It requires everything you have inside to succeed. We are all works in progress. Others only see what you have allowed them to see. You decide which version of you is being presented. A friend told me that she loves that I always show up as my true authentic self, so that is what I want for you. It's so much easier to be the truest version of yourself to overcome the challenges and adversities that are inevitable. The difference between the winners and the losers comes down to the decisions we make, having a process that works, and your commitment to following and implementing the process in your life. The goal is to manifest what you envision.

Notes under the door.

I recently talked with a coaching client. She spoke of how difficult things had been since her kids were attending school online and she was working from home. To curb her kids from interrupting her all day, she told them to write their request on a small piece of paper and slide it under her bedroom door. She is a single mother and not used to having to juggle the change that required her kids to learn at home and for her bedroom to double as an office. Her regular schedule had long gone and soon she was struggling to manage her kids, home, and everything that came with being the responsible parent. The kids began to slide notes under her door every few minutes until they went unanswered and began mounting. The more they piled up, the angrier she became. After hearing her frustration, I paused for a moment to prepare my response.

What I heard was a cry for help, but I realized what she needed was a reminder. She needed to remember that she had always controlled her home, she was the general manager of her home and family. As society changed, her role did not; how she had to do things outside of her typical routine did change. I reminded her that she could not abandon the structure that she had spent years implementing for a laxer laidback environment. The kids were screaming for structure while she was floundering looking for things to pacify them - knowing, in reality, nothing would change until she did.

Are you managing the situation rather than having it manage you? That was my question.

Hearing her explain her situation, it was clear she knew the solution but had made the choice to play the victim, instead of handling it. She chose to complain rather than making the necessary changes to correct the situation. I called her on her BS, and as she heard me say it back to her, she could do nothing but agree. As she heard me talk, all she could do was laugh. It is not that we don't know what to do, but rather we need a nudge, a reminder, and a process to stay on track. As first-generation Black women entrepreneurs, we are often charting new territory without a roadmap.

"Tell me what your routine was previously?" I asked.

It was obvious that she felt overwhelmed but hearing my response to her situation helped her understand that she stopped doing the things that helped her manage her home. She was not preparing for the day, so the day was controlling her. This is what happens in some people's lives. Because they have not taken control, they are operating by default. Just because they were not leaving the house did not mean abandoning what worked in the past. Her kids still needed her, probably more now than ever. No matter what happens, the day doesn't stop for your challenges. You must keep moving in the face of adversity, especially when the new day starts and although the goal has not changed, we must change how we go about achieving it. If we are prepared for it, it is not as hard to manage. Life can happen fast and cause us to feel the same way my client did. We often feel overwhelmed, usually because we are operating without a process, roadmap, or blueprint. Sometimes you have to take it back to the basics or the classics as I like to refer to the things that work or the things that have worked in the past. Preparation is the key; it's often said that preparation mixed with opportunity creates your luck.

Time to S.H.I.F.T.

You know, you need to let go of the past and the things that no longer fit your life. To move forward you have to lighten your load to maneuver through the bullshit that threatens to take you out of the game. By focusing on the prize and releasing the things that we no longer need we increase our odds of success. We no longer clog our minds with insignificant things that make it hard to process and act on the possibilities that lie ahead. It's time to let go to elevate. Going through this process helped me understand some of my feelings and emotions that I had not explored.

Listen, to overcome we must surrender to the present moment. This means surrendering yourself to your current circumstances. This does not mean you are giving up, quitting, or moving away from what you desire, but instead, it's more like stepping back to assess the journey rather than a full retreat. It gives you space to think about your life, the decisions you are making, and the circumstances. It helps you gather new insights and perspectives while providing space to move forward in a better way, which creates the space for positive change and transformation. When you surrender, you release all attachment to past trauma, failure, and mistakes that hold you back and often sabotage your progress. When you release and let go, you're surrendering to the present moment. You're surrendering yourself to how things are right now, and this makes way for new opportunities and perspectives.

Let me help empower and motivate you to work these steps that might change your life. It's time to get organized and move towards your goals on purpose. Ultimately, this book should serve as support to other women of color, specifically Black women, because I want us all to overcome and thrive to live our best lives. Life is full of ups and downs. One day, you may feel like you have it all figured out. Then, at a moment's notice, oh S.H.I.F.T., you realize that you don't. You're not alone in these feelings. Everyone must face their own set of challenges. Learning how to overcome challenges will help you stay centered and remain calm under pressure. Everyone has their preferences for how to face a challenge in life, however, I have found that everything does not work for everyone. You must find the process that speaks to you and your mindset. You must determine what works and what does not for your life. I have identified some tools and tips that if followed in good times and bad, will help you overcome your challenges, remove obstacles and succeed.

The following are the steps we will break down to walk you through the process and help you become the best version of yourself, the person you believe yourself to be.

The Steps to S.H.I.F.T.

1. State the problem (Identify)
2. Heal and Help yourself (accountability)
3. Identify the purpose
4. Focus
5. Trust the process

Change means doing something different and it also takes time, so patience is mandatory. You must be kind to yourself, speak life to your situation, and take the time to deal with your challenges. Persistence, practice, and a positive attitude will open doors that will change your life. No matter your situation, the hard times will happen, but with the right mindset and this process, you will be able to overcome them every time and grow in the process.

S.H.I.F.T. TIP:

It's time to give up the things that add no value to your life and where you desire to go.

SHIFT NOTES

PART TWO

The Steps

"Do the difficult things while they are easy and do the great things while they are small. A journey of a thousand miles must begin with a single step."

~Lao Tzu

CHAPTER FOUR

Ahhh S.H.I.F.T.!
Step One: State the Problem

What's Blocking you from Winning?

I recently had a light bulb moment. This was the moment when I got it. "It" is that epiphany I received that showed me the importance of identifying what I need to overcome the challenges that seem to have their foot on my neck, keeping me bound. I see the same realizations when I have a breakthrough with my coaching clients. It's the moment when you realize you already have exactly what you need to achieve your goals.

You have to ask yourself a few questions, "What's the long-term goal?" "What matters to you the most?" "What would you like to see happen in your life?"

Once we make these decisions, we must clarify the goal. Each time I'm meeting with someone, I prepare for the meeting by asking, "How do you think I can help you? I pose that question to you now. This is something you should know before we can move forward. If you do not know the answer to this question, you'll find yourself floundering looking for the right fit, rather than customizing the solution to fit your life.

We all have the power to overcome, but we have to be willing and ready to tap into it.

When you think about your purpose in life you begin to ask yourself questions like, "What am I doing?" What am I here for?

Usually, when I start those conversations with my clients, I'm asking them questions like, "How do you feel I'm going to be able to help?"

What do you need?

When faced with decisions about your life and entrepreneurial pursuits, it's your decisions that determine your possibilities or probability of success. It's important to know which direction to go. My goal is to help point you in the right direction to identify the needs for your specific journey. I may not have all the answers, but I have made enough mistakes to tell you what not to do. I also had enough wins to know how to achieve more. This process will take you being alert, focused, well-read, and prepared to step outside of the proverbial box and succeed. To overcome the challenges that threaten you. You must make meaningful life decisions that move you closer to your desired destination.

How to identify your needs:

- Ask yourself, what is most important to you?
- What do you need to achieve your desired results?

From this place, all choices, conflicts, and dilemmas, can be measured, creating a life you envision. When you know what you want to achieve it becomes easier to determine the tools you will need for your journey.

How to acquire it:

- Why do I need it?
- Where do I get it?
- Cost of acquiring it?

Now you will follow the process to get what you need to progress. By knowing "why" we need it, it helps give us context and motivates us to get it. The 'Why' should serve as your motivation to keep pursuing when you want to stop. It's really about me offering the motivation that sometimes we are unable to find in ourselves and build on that. Once we know what we need and why it matters we can begin to pinpoint the location to find it. Is it a friend, mentor, organization, or manual? Wherever it is, it's your job to find the resource. You must also remember that everything has a cost, although you may not pay in legal tender, you may pay with time, talent, or whatever the holder of the "need" deems appropriate. The more we understand our own needs, the easier it is to influence, navigate conflicts and implement initiatives successfully. Neglecting to identify and secure your needs signifies a lack of direction or self-motivation, which can create chaos in our lives and the lives of those around us. Unmet needs on the other hand can manifest in unhealthy choices that do not help you overcome to move closer to your desired destination. Those of us with the need for growth must focus on learning and developing new talents, skills, and ways of overcoming. Uncertainty comes with blazing your trail. You must let go of what was, to navigate this new phase of your life.

You gotta have you.

It is your responsibility to identify and fill your need, rather than expecting others to do this work for you. Making your needs the responsibility of someone else leads to us blaming everything and everyone else for our lack of progress and inability to overcome and succeed. Being aware and practicing finding a way to meet your own needs and values is a powerful tool that enhances self-leadership and empowerment, creating the life and career we each desire. This is a crucial component of your solution as you must know what you need. Although it sounds simple, it's often overlooked.

Experience is the best teacher.

Since my kids were small, when they made a mistake or did something wrong, I was never the parent to say, "Oh God, why did you do that?!" That question seemed pointless because if we knew the outcome, we wouldn't do half the things we do, especially as kids. Instead, I ask, "What did you learn from this experience?"

I want to make sure you understand what you've got to look at. We all have made mistakes and as long as we are living, we'll make more. The key is to learn from the mistake and use that lesson to realize a growth opportunity. When you look back at a situation in hindsight it's always easier to see the error of our ways if we pay attention and are honest with ourselves. Maybe there is something we could have or should have done differently or sooner. This is the work that you have to do with yourself because we all can move through challenges.

From a therapeutic side, it's really about having the right coping skills to get through anything, no matter the situation. What helped me understand the lesson was what I learned from each situation.

Along the process, there are always many different emotions. There are always going to be the six basic emotions: anger, disgust, fear, happiness, sadness, and surprise. Although there are about 27 different emotions, people get stuck on a few, like "I'm sad" or "I'm happy." It's important to understand that emotions are more than just feelings, they help dictate our mindset which dictates our actions. By understanding that what you are feeling is normal, but should be felt, explored, addressed, and cleared to move forward. This is the space where peace arrives. If we allow our emotions to control us, we will find ourselves removed from any resemblance of peace stuck once again. Knowing how to navigate your journey is one of the leading components of your success. The lack of that knowledge hampers many from achieving those successes.

My mom taught me a valuable lesson that prepared me for life and removed any fear I had of asking questions. She would say, "Don't ever be afraid to ask me anything. The answer is only going to be yes or no. Asking these questions takes you out of your comfort zone. Once we identify the needs, then we must locate the people who can support the need. Relationships are critical. Networking and making connections outside of your immediate sphere of influence will help identify the need. I learned that you never want to be the smartest person in your circle because your chances of learning something new diminishes. I tapped the resources, learned as much as I could, and took advantage of the opportunity that these connections presented. This process provided the answers I needed and got me to the next level of my journey.

Emotional IQ.

My emotional development has been a part of my journey here. Early in my life, I suppressed emotions for a long time because I knew how emotional I was, hence, the reason I call myself "The Crybaby". I get emotional because I can feel so much. I empathize strongly as I genuinely want people to overcome their situations to win. When I think back over my trials and challenges, I'm filled with good emotions that turn to tears of joy. I've been working on the art of self-healing with my wellness coach and learned that it's about accepting that I'm emotional. It is what it is. I might tear up for a few moments, catch my breath, and then I'm going to keep it moving.

It starts with you knowing who you are. Many of the women I coach may have this idea, but don't know the steps or how to begin. What they do have is a vision of what they would like to accomplish. For example, I've met many people that have told me they wanted to open a group home. I believe they tell me, because they know I own a few and have successfully operated them for over fifteen years. As a coach, I would say they are doing the right thing by seeking answers from someone who has already been where you are attempting to go. The thing you must remember before approaching someone for help is that you must do your research and be prepared to answer basic questions about your vision. If you cannot answer basic questions like, "what kind of group home? What population will you serve? Where would you like to be located?" If they cannot answer those basic questions. In that instant, it shows me that you have not taken the time to process your vision, do your homework, and because you have not defined a population you do not even know who you will sell this service to. It's easy to say you want it but are you willing to do the work to get it. I believe many are infatuated with the idea that being self-employed is sexy, so they focus on that part and miss the real work. We worship this idea of being independent but don't see the dirty, nonstop work-make-you-wanna-holler side of it. They become infatuated with that facade, but when you investigate deeper, there's no substance to their vision. This makes identifying your true needs impossible because there are no needs in the land of make-believe.

With each venture I've begun, I have always done my research. For me and my life, there are no excuses, just results. I do not believe in taking myself off the hook with an excuse, which translates to I was not prepared. When I decided what I wanted, I was working on my master's degree. I was working a full-time job. I was also a married mother of three. It was a difficult time that I dealt with, going into full action mode. I used what I did not want to see in my life as a motivation to identify what I needed and act on that.

I began compiling a list of what I needed by doing what I call, following the leaders. This meant I would find a job with the largest supplier of the services I wanted to offer, understand their structure and learn their process. This would help me pinpoint the need and create a roadmap to guide me on my journey. I learned their policy, procedures, forms, templates, and overall information. I was just gathering information. And then they would have these informational meetings once a month or every third month or whatever. I went to these meetings and then I met a couple of ladies that were willing to share some of the pieces that probably would have been missing if I didn't ask for the help I needed.

I always hear my mother saying, "they can only say yes or no."

The blueprint.

These are the nuggets of wisdom I've gained along the way. An accumulation of all the valuable lessons I have received. The wisdom and lessons did not come from one person. It's from brainstorming sessions, masterminds, and conversations. A peer of mine and I were actually in the same business and anytime she called me, she would say, "I just love you. I love talking to you because you motivate me. You encourage me. You're empowering..." She would say all the positive things that you could think of. What I learned over the few years that I had known her was that sometimes she just needed to vent, and she didn't have anybody that would listen to her, because her business partner was her best friend. I would just listen. There wasn't anything that I needed to add. But I think as she talked to me and talked through the things that she would have going on, she was figuring it out. She was open to the idea, but once I called her out on her stuff, she sat in the car for two hours crying. She was having a full range of the emotional spectrum. All these different emotions and feelings began to surface.

She was using me to fill one of her "needs" I was providing the motivation she needed to continue. She could not speak to her partner, so I was the next in line. I accepted the challenge and she confided in me. I could tell after our conversations she was much lighter and relaxed.

The secret sauce.

We often already have what we need, but just need someone to help pull it out of us. I hope that this book will serve as the catalyst or the stepping stone to help you start that process. So I had to make it more structured and more intentional so that people could get what they needed and walk away with something good.

S.H.I.F.T. TIP:

Take inventory of your resources and never be afraid to ask for help to fill the gaps.

"Believe in the power of truth," she told them. "Do not allow your mind to be imprisoned by majority thinking."

~Dr. Patricia E. Bath

SHIFT NOTES

"Women, if the soul of the nation is to be saved, I believe that you must become its soul."

~Coretta Scott King

CHAPTER FIVE

I'm the S.H.I.F.T.!
Step Two: Heal & Help Yourself
You've Got the Power!

Have you ever thought about how your life would be affected by not accomplishing your life goals? Have you thought about the people and the events your decision may affect? Most have not, but I say that to remind you that it's bigger than you. Your destiny is not your own as it's tied to the people that are waiting on you to do what you were designed to do. That action just may free someone you haven't even met yet. How do you plan on overcoming your obstacles to achieve your goals?

I made a promise to myself several years ago. The promise was that I would achieve my goals no matter what challenges stood in my path. If you are not willing to make promises to yourself that you keep, then you are wasting your time with this book. This is not meant to be a complicated exercise, but rather affirming what you want to manifest. I promised myself to always be and do my best, so that's what I did.

When I read my promise, it makes me feel like I've got my own back. I'm accountable to myself. If I'm not, I fail before I start. I keep the things that inspire me at the forefront of my mind. You have big goals, you must stay the course to achieve them. If what you needed to accomplish happened instantly, then you wouldn't have to worry about how to stay accountable, you would just get it done. Looking at what's ahead may feel like an overwhelming mission ahead of you, but thinking big requires big action. If they were something you could easily accomplish overnight, then you wouldn't have to worry about how to stay accountable, you would just get it done.

Most of us struggle with the day-to-day details and the habits that rob us of our time, ambition, and focus. We often trade the habits that help us achieve our goals, with habits that keep us stuck or stagnant. The bottom line is, no matter how motivated you get, strategic action is what wins games. You must hold yourself accountable for the choices you make and the consequences they bring. While there are some instances where things are out of your control, how you respond to those circumstances and how you decide to approach all the other situations that are in your control is entirely up to you. We do not live in an ideal world, there are rarely perfect circumstances, and many things are not in our control. You still can make the best decisions possible within your given circumstances and focus on the things you can control to make the best choices possible.

S.H.I.F.T. time!

When you are stuck in a rut, you have to make a shift. The shift is getting the information and the resources you need so that you can get to the next level, the next thing that you're trying to do or accomplish. I probably say it happened for me around forty. I started to emerge from my rut when I was going through my divorce. I finally realized that I could not, nor should I try to be all things to everybody. For so many years I was accountable for everyone else. Although I was the baby in the family, I had the most responsibility. That was a lot to carry. Being responsible for everyone else helped me see what I wanted for my life, but I knew accountability to myself would be the difference between me succeeding or not. I had seen what not being accountable had done to my siblings. I had to be my checks and balances, and not allow myself to slide, get by, do just enough, or be derailed from my route.

You have choices that only you can make for yourself. I have to do everything for myself, so I embrace the mantra, Failure is not an option for me. Author, Alice Walker said, "The most common way people give up their power is by thinking they don't have any." You must remind yourself that you always have power, but if you think you don't, you won't. It's that simple.

Ownership is owning every situation, and that comes with self-reflection, you know, when I talk to my kids, maybe they had a test but didn't do well on it. I would say, “Based on my observation, I didn’t see you put your all into studying.” They usually say, “Yeah mom you’re right, I probably should have studied a little bit more or I could have gone to a group study. After that, they usually shift and turn the grade around, doing what they know they should have done the first time and end up doing well.

We must also be accountable for the words we speak as the power of life and death lies in the tongue. Once you speak something into the atmosphere and believe it, it must happen. It’s a universal principle, similar to the Law of Attraction. The thought, idea, or whatever was verbalized takes a life of its own, therefore you must be mindful about what you say.

For so long, I guess you could say I was not living in my truth. I was not who I was created to be because I wanted to be accepted. I again dimmed my light to fit the status quo. I think that I muffled myself, my words, or didn't freely be who I am. I'm a daydreamer, meaning I can just be off and think, usually when I'm meditating. This is when I imagine what or how I want things to be and then I just keep working towards what I visualized or what I have written down as a goal.

When I dare to be powerful, to use my strength in the service of my vision, then it becomes less and less important whether I am afraid to act. I have to make the decision that fear is not something I entertain. There's no place for fear in survival mode. Winning is the objective, one wrong move and things could not go how you want them to go. I manage a million-dollar budget for my business in addition to trying to keep up with my household. If I fail there are serious repercussions. But you can't focus on what could go wrong, instead think about the possibilities to avoid getting stuck. You cannot allow negative thoughts to infiltrate your mind. You must eliminate the naysayers and the negativity, or you'll find yourself focused on the wrong things. We can't control other people or things, but we can control ourselves.

Accountability has never been something I struggled with. I learned this at an early age dealing with siblings who are addicts. Seeing them never hold themselves accountable showed me how ridiculous it was to not have that piece. Accountability begins by adjusting your attitude from a victim mentality to an empowered mindset. When you understand that every choice has a consequence, you're more careful about the decisions you make. True long-term change comes from long-term efforts. Failing is a part of the process, but it's not the end. Once you fail you must be able to lift yourself and continue to put one foot in front of the other, in other words, keep stepping. No pain, no gain is what the song says. I would take it a step further to say even when you experience gain, it's just the beginning.

I needed to be strong and face my truths, which often meant answering tough questions about who I am and what I am willing and not willing to sacrifice along the way. I learned a long time ago that investing in myself was important and worth all the time, money, and effort. Some investments pan out immediately, but others take longer to adjust, correct, and perform. Patience is the key, but while you wait it's imperative you do the work to stay the course. Once you have decided you are worth the effort it's time to do the work that's required. You cannot hold yourself accountable if you do not know what your objectives are.

You must know exactly what you want to accomplish. You also need to know why it's important to you. When you know the motivation behind the action it hits a little differently and moves you to action. On any given day, I'm human resources, payroll, mediator, and CEO to name a few of the hats I wear. If there is a hat to be worn, I'm wearing it or have worn it at some point. That's a reality that I have to accept and embrace. I knew that was a requirement for me to reach the level of success. Ask yourself how are you going to prepare for that? Things will not always go the way you envision so you must be prepared.

Losing my mom at an early age forced me to be independent. She had taught me what it meant to be resilient and take care of myself. So, the combination pushed me to thrive even when it looked impossible. I think I set myself up to not be told no. When that happens, it sparks something inside of me that says I must get a yes. I feel like I work just as hard. My money is just like everyone else's, green. I should be able to do whatever I want to do.

Staying focused on what you can do is the most important thing, you don't make progress by standing on the sidelines whimpering and complaining. Sometimes people allow things to frustrate them. You can't carry that. Because it will hold you down.

S.H.I.F.T. TIP:

You have to find the power and resources to change the trajectory of your life.

SHIFT NOTES

*"Write the vision,
make it plain."*

~God

CHAPTER SIX

Talk That S.H.I.F.T.!
Step Three: Identify Your Purpose
Intentionally Inspired

We all are created for a purpose. We all have skills and talents that are unique to us. If life's a game, It takes strategy to overpower your opponent. Your biggest opponent is not the people talking behind your back or the person looking at you with a side-eye, it's yourself. We are our harshest critics, worst self-sabotagers, and blockers of our own blessings. So, a huge part of your plan must include a strategy to overcome you. Your plan is the foundation of your goal. Without a plan, you have no way of reaching your goal. The plan is how you're going to get to the goal. So, if you're mapping that out, you're able to see the ending in your mind. My plan has evolved. Today I'm more intentional than I have ever been. I put more thought into planning now because it makes my life simpler. Planning has helped me avoid stress, it keeps the process moving forward and ultimately increases my chances of success.

It's normal for me to have multiple projects going on at once. I'm making several things happen at the same time, which doesn't happen by default. My planning process is unique as I imagine yours will be as well. We often get caught up in the idea that it has to look a certain way, be in a certain format or font, but the plan that I'm talking about is your blueprint to achieve your goals. It may seem weird, but I can be anywhere or at any time and I'm working on my plan. I can be in the line at the bank, mapping out my next steps. When my mind says go, I must capture the idea, thought, process, challenge, method, or message, so I will record messages on my phone, text myself, or type it in my notes program. The key is I have to capture it and use it to build my plan. We are not using this plan to apply for bank funding, but rather get the biggest return on our investment in ourselves.

When responsibilities grow and life happens, we tend to lose focus and get off track. Understandably, the issue that is the most urgent requires the most attention, but we tell ourselves what's "urgent" to us. You have to ask yourself...are you making planning out your life and business an urgency?

Using this process helps me stay organized, saves me time, and gets it out of my head, which is necessary to function at my best, which is focused on achieving the goal. I see things in black or white, meaning it's yes or no, go or stop, there is no grey or slow down. Each day I ask myself, "What didn't I complete today?" Whatever it is will be at the top of my list tomorrow. I'm realistic about my expectations for my life and have to plan accordingly and set realistic goals so I am not overwhelmed or burnt out.

Planning is a daily process that must fit your schedule. I'm visual, so I have to do what works best for me. You must do what works for you. I use my Google Calendars and notebooks to track ideas, appointments, and things to do. Now it is just a matter of going through the process and making the progress required to stay on track to achieve the goal. Sometimes we become so technical that people cannot see how the process can be applied to our lives to promote our growth. But life happens, we get caught up and never go back to take time to do the work required to complete the plan. When something doesn't go the way that you anticipate it going, you know, something happens, somebody passes away, you have a car accident or one of your girlfriends is not feeling well, however life happens. These are just moments in time, if you sit in that, you get stuck. You must have the mindset that this is something that I am going through. It is not who I am. It is a part of the process. You must go through it to get to it.

There's not one big plan. But multiple plans that you must have. You have to plan for your business, for your physical health plan for mental well-being, and your spiritual plan. For each part of your life to thrive, you must have a strategy that gets you from where you are to where you want to be. You have to develop goals and create timelines for completing those goals in each category. You must revisit your plan and goals daily, journal about your desires each night, and regularly set aside moments to visualize what you want. This helps you to schedule your next steps. You may need to review weekly or monthly depending on your timeline to completion and your schedule. The goal is to figure out the best way to make it work for you.

People usually jumble everything together, not realizing that they do have to separate it so that it can be real. If you are trying to do all things at one time, something is going to end up not getting done or not getting the attention that it needs. If you separate it into different compartments, then you can address that particular thing and track your progress much easier. Now you begin to have small accomplishments as you go along the way, which you must remember to celebrate.

The planning process has been instrumental to the growth of my business. I am in tune with my process. I know when I need to pivot or make something happen. These are the needed adjustments that keep your plan from becoming outdated and obsolete. So, the plan is not the original, but a modified version to accommodate the pivot that needed to happen and keep you on track. I now find myself constantly getting new information, ideas and opportunities.

Mission accomplished.

When I decided to close one of my locations, it was not an easy decision, but it was strategic. I felt like I had accomplished the goal that I had set out to do, which was to open three facilities within three years, instead, I did it in eighteen months. I had put enough work and energy into that venture at that particular time, so I did not consider that a loss. I knew that part of my plan required me to transition. I could have decided not to make that transition, but I would have continued to be stressed about it. For me, it's always about moving forward in my life. As I get older, I think about working smarter, not harder. I must continue to learn the required lessons and apply them in the process.

When I decided to close the third location. I had to go into action planning mode. I decided the date we would close, determined placement for clients, began working with case managers and everyone involved to make the transition as smooth as possible. To prepare for the conversations with each of the families and the clients we care for I made what in my industry they call social stories, which is a great tool for my clients who happen to be autistic. I created stories about them getting ready to move to the new location. I showed them images of the people you're going to see, the place you are going to, what your new room will look like, and when it's going to happen. Then the family picks the client up, takes them to visit the facility. This makes for a smooth transition.

Everything related to my work is all about planning. The work that I do every day is about making transitions smooth. Some of this is an intuition for me, but if it is not for you, do not worry. Repetition creates habit and if practiced just right can yield big results. Everything that I do is always about planning and making sure, especially for my clients, that their needs are being met. I think the biggest cost that will be required is not only monetarily, but your time.

The perfect time.

I have learned that waiting for the right moment is not a real thing, you must seize each moment. When I have an idea about something or like it is just in my spirit and I know that if I put my mind to it, I'm going to be able to accomplish it. What I've learned recently is that I might not accomplish it in the time that I want to accomplish it, but if I'm working towards it, it's going to happen.

I have always wanted to do better, to have more, to be more sustained. So, in all of those things, success is the result of planning and making the effort. You can see what the outcome will be. That's the process. Knowing that something is waiting for you on the other side of this plan is motivating for me. The willingness to know that it's going to be a process and that it is not going to happen overnight keeps you on track to get to the next level.

I am a template to follow, not because I've done everything right, but instead I've been where you may be attempting to go. I have also made mistakes, that if avoided can save you the pain and setbacks I experienced. I had been using this process for years before I realized that it was a process. I was figuring out what worked along the way before I realized what I was doing.

By making it as plain as possible, to cut through the BS, it can fit your life and become real. The planning is merely about creating goals, steps, and deadlines. This answers what and how which alone can change your perspective and your life will follow. Having a blueprint increases your odds of success. By doing these five steps, you will be able to get to the next level and then the next level quicker.

Social stories coaching.

I have learned to apply this skill to many of my coaching clients to assist them with their planning process. Think about seeing yourself in the story. Imagine describing the situation you desire to see yourself in. You are the main character in this story and it's all about you and your transition. Where are you going and what does it look like there? Visualizing what things you will need and seeing yourself with all of those things. See yourself overcoming the challenge and embrace that feeling. As the process and transition may be difficult, this can help you to understand it, step by step.

S.H.I.F.T. TIP:

It's time to give up the things that have no purpose.

SHIFT NOTES

Clarindria Addison

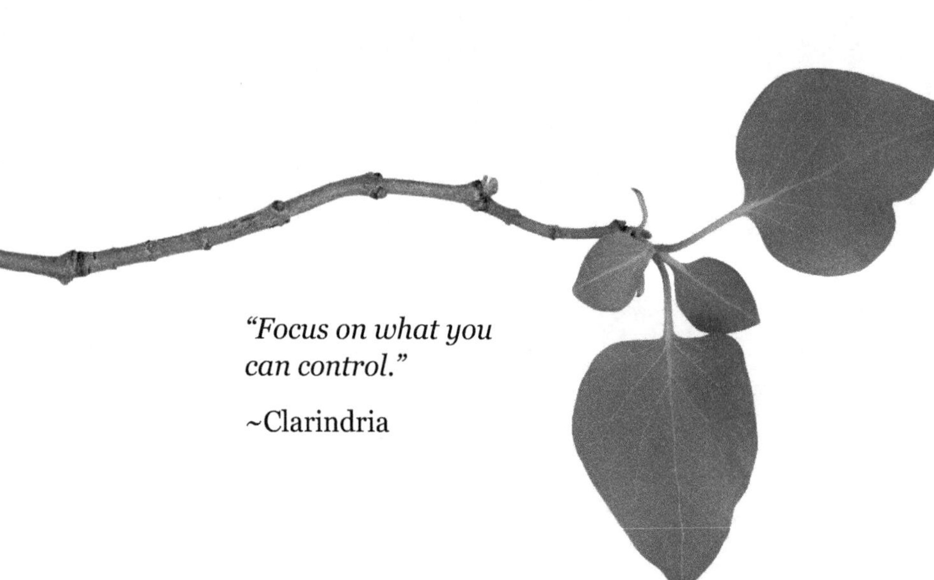

"Focus on what you can control."

~Clarindria

CHAPTER SEVEN

New S.H.I.F.T.
Step Four: Focus on What Matters
Game Changed!

What if I told you that you could feel more positive and in control of your entire life if you focus on what you wanted to achieve and how you wanted to achieve it? If you've ever tried to focus on one thing for an extended period, you know that is easier than it sounds. When I identified my target. It was similar to waking up from my coma. When I began to focus my life took flight. I developed clarity, reduced my stress, and my business grew.

To concentrate on one thing you must, by default, ignore many other things. Living in a noisy world with distractions makes focusing even more difficult even more challenging. Things tend to pop up and cause us to lose focus. These distractions make concentrating on your interest hard. But knowing what's important in your life and aiming to achieve it will determine your level of success. This requires you to be able to pay attention to your plan and control the everyday distractions that life puts in your path.

Think about it like this, focus happens when you choose to push the other things to the back. You must eliminate the things that have the potential to distract you from focusing on the vision for the future. This doesn't mean you can never do all the things you want to do, it just means you cannot do them all right now at the same damn time. You must prioritize the things you'd like to do to make sure you aren't doing that ahead of something you may need to do. You always have options, but if you want to succeed, the key is focusing on one thing at a time to achieve your goal. Would you want your heart surgeon thinking about chopping down a tree while he's operating on you?

Shortlist people are more focused.

To find this focus that eludes many, you must understand the concept of baby steps. Doing and focusing on one thing first allows you to get to the next thing. This requires a very shortlist. As you begin to check things off of your shortlist you are inspired to do more. On the other hand, when you make a larger list, it creates chaos and confusion in your mind because it appears to be overwhelming. Your brain shuts down and you don't know where to start. You must first figure out what matters most and create steps on how you plan to achieve it. This process must be intentional. When you're choosing something to work on, you should be choosing one thing at a time. It's easy to get overwhelmed when you have a list of twenty things to accomplish. When you're attempting to tackle twenty things, you'll realize there are not enough hours in the day to get it all done. Not completing the list has a way of demotivating you and causing you to lose focus once again. Without focus, you're lost, anxious, disappointed and you've wasted so much time.

If you feel like you are all over the place you're not alone. Many women, who are just like you, struggle with narrowing down their focus. I like to say it's not because we're confused, but because we're brilliant beyond measure. You want to accomplish so much as you feel the pressure to be every woman. The key is to harness and control that brilliance to make it a benefit rather than a hindrance.

When the goal is what you must look forward to if you do X, Y and Z, this makes the vision tangible. Now imagine if you put a deadline on it and only did that for the next four weeks for example. You have defined what you are going to accomplish and added a timeline to keep you on track and accountable. That's something that you can put your hands on and doing the work is going to get you there. Throughout my life, there have been times that I have not been focused, but I have been able to win by finding my focus. I have always been the type of person that did not like to sit and fester in any place for a long time. Going through my divorce, I felt like I was working through the steps. It was like a part of me had died, so to overcome it, I had to go through the grief process. I had to talk about what I was experiencing with people I trusted, accept my feelings, take care of my children as well as myself, connect with others who could relate, and remember to celebrate my independence. This process got me through. I was able to overcome it. Even though I had all of those feelings, I knew that I was going to be a better me not being in that situation.

I asked myself an important question. I wanted to know what it would take to be a better me. I knew I wanted to be the healthiest version of myself, mind, body, and spirit. I knew that I wanted to build a business that would serve as a legacy to my children. So, I went to work. I began working out, eating healthier, and doing all the things that the research showed to work. I was focused on being the best version of myself. I lost weight, built multiple businesses and seven years later I found myself on a self-healing journey that has allowed me to focus even more.

Stuck in a rut.

Some people may get stuck in the situation of what's happening and are not able to move past it, mainly because they are not focused on what coming out of that situation looks like. For whatever reason, their sights are not set on the steps to move them from where they are to where they want to be. They don't see the prize that awaits them on the other side, instead, they are stuck in that moment versus accepting the moment for what it was and seeing past it. For me, it’s about reaching my destination. It was never about dabbling here or there with things that were not a part of my purpose or plan. Being spread thin or bouncing all over the place is a sure-fire way to failure. When you begin to understand that focus gives life to your purpose it provides direction and something to work on. The fact is, focusing on and implementing this process will help you get to the next level. Don’t misunderstand, there is work and commitment that will be required. True, it’s not realistic that you will be focused during every situation or encounter. Distractions will come and when they do you must be prepared and not lose focus. Losing your focus can take you on a detour and cause you to lose your way. Focusing your thoughts gets you back on the right route, just as a GPS System re-centers you to get you back on track to your destination.

Choose your focus.

Early in my career, I worked for an organization called Wraparound Milwaukee, which was a unique system of care for children with serious emotional, behavioral, and mental health needs and their families. It utilized a wraparound philosophy and approach which focused on strength-based, individualized care. There I learned about the importance of focusing on being positive and pulling emotions, feelings, information out of people, giving them a space to deal with the things inside of them. The results and success rate were amazing. I believe the secret was not a secret at all, they just realized the clients were stuck in a cycle of negativity, not seeing the positive things in their lives. They shared a simple truth that states: We could all be doing something better, have more or an easier route, but we are still here, standing at this moment with another opportunity to fix it, build it, or just make it right.

Learning to focus helped me immensely. Before my brother got clean from drugs, he was stuck in his story, so much that I knew it verbatim. "I worked at UPS for 30 years...I used to travel all the time...I had a Corvette..." But that was in the past. That story was no longer benefiting him. He had become a drug addict, without a home, sleeping on someone's couch, not taking showers. He did drive a Corvette several years ago, but now he did not have money to get on the bus. He was stuck using what used to be a crutch because what was happening in the present was crippling. He was using his past to prop himself up, but it was useless because he was only fooling himself. Even Though my brother was someone I used to look up to, that conversation of the past had no value now and was not going to affect his current situation nor his future. The fact was he was a drug addict that needed to get clean and reliving the stories of yesterday would do nothing to help overcome his demons. He had to focus on changing his situation.

(*Don't tell me what you used to do, or used to say, unless it affects your future pay. -JayZ*)

I had to stop that narrative and remind him of what was happening. He was asking me for more money and I could not keep enabling him. Sometimes you have to have a "Come to Jesus moment" when you have butt naked honesty (I call it Butt Naked honesty because that's with no filter or sugar-coating) with yourself. I told him he had to figure this out. I could not keep enabling him. I could not keep watching him kill himself.

My brother went to treatment, let go of his story, and got off drugs. He has been clean for eight years. He is now helping with the business, and he says that having that conversation with me was one of the pieces that changed it for him.

His life changed when he decided to focus on what he wanted, rather than what he did not want to happen. That decision to shift his focus changed his life forever. Now in Alcoholics Anonymous, he was focused on the steps that would keep him clean and on the right track.

I have gone to so many AA meetings with my siblings and helped them through the program that I know the steps by heart. As I sat to write this I began to wonder if some of those principles stuck and became a part of my process to stay focused and not succumb to the distractions that I watched derail the people around me.

Each AA meeting is usually closed with everyone reciting a prayer or meditation, known as "the AA prayer" or the "Serenity Prayer." It stuck with me and became a part of my routine when I began to lose my focus. It reads:

God grant me the serenity
To accept the things I cannot change;
Courage to change the things I can;
And wisdom to know the difference.

Your come to Jesus moment.

This is in no way an altar call, but rather calling you out. What are you holding on to that needs to be released? You may be holding on to something that helped you in the past, but no longer serves you and should be released. The things that leave us stuck and bound must be released. Instead of living in his story, my brother began to stand on his story. He used it as the step he needed to overcome his challenges.

You must understand that some things are out of your control. So, the key is to focus on what you can control. If you do that, seventy-five percent of the battle is won. Everything else is up to the order of the universe and happenstance, how things were supposed to be anyway.

S.H.I.F.T. TIP:

Remember to seek progress, not perfection.

SHIFT NOTES

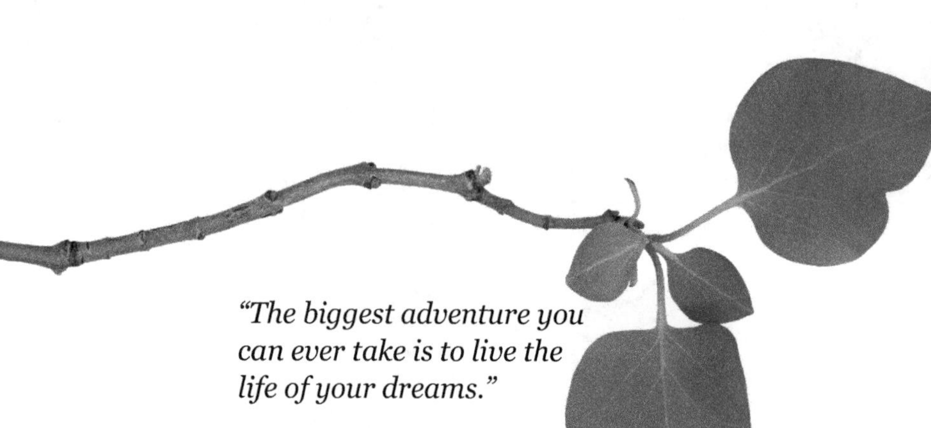

"The biggest adventure you can ever take is to live the life of your dreams."

~Oprah Winfrey

CHAPTER EIGHT

Give a S.H.I.F.T.
Step Five: Trust the Process

Believing What You Can't See

Before I embarked on the journey to overcoming my challenges to succeed. I had to envision the journey. There were so many experiences and lessons that stand out in my mind, each one has helped me in a part of my life. After reading The Purpose Driven Life, by Rick Warren, I knew I was on an intentional journey. All of these things were a part of that process that increased the odds of success. Like the title of the book, I believe my journey is purposeful and I could not have done anything differently to get to where I am now.

In my mind, I was going through these experiences, but I didn't even realize what the journey was going to be. One of my favorite scriptures is, Psalm 46:10-11 “Be still, and know that I am God! For a long time, I didn't understand why. It wasn’t until recently I realized I tend to just go, go, go like I had it all figured out. But, I was figuring it out as I traveled along the path.

Before any journey, there are a few essentials you need. These are the things that helped me to get on and stay on course. The first thing I learned was the importance of self-care. Taking the time to make sure I was ok allowed me to be the best person that I can be for the journey. In the morning, I wake up intentionally, excited about beginning my ten-minute meditation by spending time in the moment. I wake up in appreciation of the universe for allowing me to see another day. The fact that I woke up confirms that I have more work to do. I write in my journal, make my tea, and get my day going. At nighttime, I have a similar routine to wind down the day.

I'm thinking about how I want tomorrow to look, envisioning myself completing things that need to be done and visualizing those things that I want to manifest.

The power of positivity.

I learned the importance of creating positive life experiences from reading the book, *The Secret*. I came across the book several years ago and fell in love. I read it several times as it resonated with my spirit and I had seen it work. I loved it so much that I purchased multiple copies for my employees and made it required reading. Some of the things the author spoke of were things I had been doing by default, not knowing it had a name. For me, the book affirmed that well-being truly begins with believing in yourself, something I've had to do my entire life. We all have the power within to discover our life goals and purpose, and consistent affirmations keep you motivated and focused on following a blueprint designed to help achieve your dreams. As you move through these pages, stop to assess the moment, and tell yourself that you have the power in your mind to be anything and everything you want to be in this world. Remind yourself that your thoughts dictate your present and future destiny. You must apply the lessons because no one can do it for you. Success doesn't come to those who wait, but rather those who take it.

Whenever I struggle, I look at the reminders on my wall, phone, or wherever they are. I stop whatever I am doing, take a minute, even if I'm in my car, I pull over. I take five minutes to just breathe. I know that that is how I've been getting through. Now I'm able to separate the work from the rest. I know what burnout feels like and never want to be in that space again. When I was ten, I wanted to be a lawyer when I grew up mainly because people around me would say I liked to argue. I did not start to think about it until high school, but my family was grooming me for college. I would become the first person in my immediate family to go to college.

Being Led.

I went away to school in New Orleans at Xavier, but I was only there a semester before I headed back home. I quickly grew homesick as it was like I was forgotten. As all my roommates were getting their mail from loved ones, I never received anything. Again, I was the first person in my family to take this journey and no one knew how to support me or what I would need. I don't fault anybody for that. That was my family and my life.

I returned home to attend a local college to enroll in their associate program. It was a two-year liberal arts program where you go there for two years and then you transition to a four-year institution. I received my bachelor's in educational policies and community studies in 2004. I thought I was going to be a social worker.

While my mother was my rock, who became my best friend before she passed. My father and I, on the other hand, had a relationship that was predicated on his and my mother's relationship and how they got along. I often refer to him as the donor. My father was a functional alcoholic. He was brilliant, but he was also a weekend alcoholic and absent for most of my life. Our relationship was a rollercoaster ride of emotion. He had stuff he never dealt with, which caused a wedge in whatever relationship we could have had. There were several things that I learned from our relationship, mostly lessons on what not to do, but they became a part of my journey that I had to accept and use to push me further.

While I liked some of the aspects of social work, it didn't seem like what I would be doing matched what I thought I should be doing. I was in my head thinking too much, which is probably how I ended up with a Masters degree in mental health. I’ve always been a thinker and I have always worked hard. I’ve had two or three jobs since I was fifteen years old. I have not stopped. I want to make sure that there is no misunderstanding. You must understand that this is not about overnight success, but rather blood, sweat, and years of moves that ultimately led me to the path that I choose to accelerate on.

I didn't just wake up like this, with flexibility in my schedule, being able to work from anywhere, multiple businesses, and traveling constantly. No, instead I created a plan of action that helped me to see the forest through the trees. While others were blinded by what was in front of them, I was seeing the entire forest and creating a strategy for my next move.

Learning as you grow.

I get presented with opportunities all the time. But for me, I'm at a place in my life where I feel like I want to do things that are conducive to how I want to live my life. As Diamond from the movie *Players Club* once said, "Make money, don't let it make you." My hustle is universal and has ranged from cooking for restaurants, managing group homes, strategic planning, teaching, coaching, consulting to owning and running a trucking company. At each phase of my journey, I've been able to navigate my path to success. There are different levels of the journey. There's always a starting point, but when you identify more, you have to figure out how to get there. It's like a graduation of sorts. My goal now is to retire in fifteen years with a substantial nest egg, so that I can continue to live my life.

This is a process. There are going to be some things that get in the way, but as long as you stay the course, you'll be able to reach your destination. What helped me stay the course was just knowing that the goal was to succeed. Often people will have their parents or family or someone that they can kind of reach out to, but I didn't have that. Instead, I have people that depend on me to always have the answers. throughout the process.

Even Though I never learned to play chess, I made sure that my kids knew how to play. I knew the importance of strategic moves and planning. Although I never learned, I knew it was something they needed in their toolkit. Throughout my life, I've always been exposed to things that helped me grow physically, mentally, or spiritually. The exposure has provided insight into things that have opened doors and empowered me to walk through them.

I had a blueprint because I compiled it. No one gave it to me, but instead, they shared the lessons and I listened. I soaked up all the knowledge I could and put the blueprint together using what I learned.

Many people mistakenly think this was easy or that it happened overnight. Before it was my blueprint, it was my maybe it will work, or I think I should do that. It was a series of trial and error that sometimes worked and at other times it did not. The times it didn't work would be considered as failures for most, but for me, they were just wrong turns that needed to be corrected to get me back on course. By being in tune and using what has become my process, I've been able to overcome failures that could have destroyed me.

I have never accepted no for an answer. Instead, I would just work to figure out how to get to a "yes."

When I decided to open the group home for teen moms, I had spent hours doing tons of research, went to planning and zoning meetings, and completed a long laundry list of requirements to have my house approved to start the process. When it was time to present my project to the City Zoning Board, I realized that the City had a twenty-five-hundred square foot rule. This meant no other group home could be within twenty-five-hundred square feet of another.

I did not know that until after I submitted the paperwork and got through the process. I was almost ready to give up, but I decided to do more research and discovered a loophole. If I was able to get the support of my Alderman, I was more than likely to have my project approved. At the time the Alderman in my district was someone I was familiar with, and he had a reputation of being a sensible man of the people. I set up a meeting with him and together we walked the neighborhood. I joined the neighborhood committee and he showed me how to become a part of the fabric of the community.

Next, I needed to go to the meetings and let the committee who approves my request know that we were going to be a part of the community, not just have this business there. We had a plan to be a support and hire people from within the community. All those good things got us the approval we needed.

Sure, this could have played out multiple ways. I spent more money to purchase a home in another neighborhood, but more importantly, I almost gave up. The decision I made to not stop has saved me on multiple occasions throughout my life. I knew of people that had done what I was trying to do. I also believed that I was capable and passionate about the project. It was not something I just woke up and wanted to do because it was trendy. Instead, it was something I truly cared about. I knew the demographic I was serving needed what I was preparing to provide.

By this time, I had been researching for two years. I wanted to learn all I could to increase the odds of the project's success. At that time, I was volunteering in a group home for Teen Moms to get as much experience as I could. I could not understand how a teen girl would get pregnant and their mom, grandmother, or boyfriend would put them out on the streets to fend for themselves. I knew there was a need, and I knew I could be beneficial to help fill the need that existed, so I was determined to achieve the goal, by any means necessary. Many people start projects without doing the required due diligence, which often leaves them unprepared and decreases the chances for success. Going in without the proper preparation, knowledge or insight can make for a costly lesson.

I get an average of three to five calls a week from people who want to know how to open a group home. I can now tell them that I have the blueprint and begin asking the questions that they need to answer to position themselves for success. No, I don’t know all the answers, but I do know it’s possible and I can help. If the people interested in following my blueprint were doing it solely for the money, I would advise them that they needed to rethink their motives. I didn't get paid for the first six or seven months. So, passion pulled me in and that’s what also kept me. I knew that if I had the patience and stayed the course, I would be able to reap the benefits of my labor. For me, it wasn't about how much money I was going to make. I wanted to help the young ladies overcome their obstacles as well.

We knew we wanted to do things differently to disrupt the status quo. We got the ladies' hair and nails done and did other activities to provide exposure and opportunities that they may not have had access to in their current environment. Seeing this manifest brought joy to my heart. For the young ladies to see that someone had their back and was supporting them was invaluable. This was not something they were used to. My sight allowed me to see beyond what was on the surface to tackle the turmoil that existed inside of them.

S.H.I.F.T. TIP:

Believe that there is a method to the madness that you have the secret code to overcome.

SHIFT NOTES

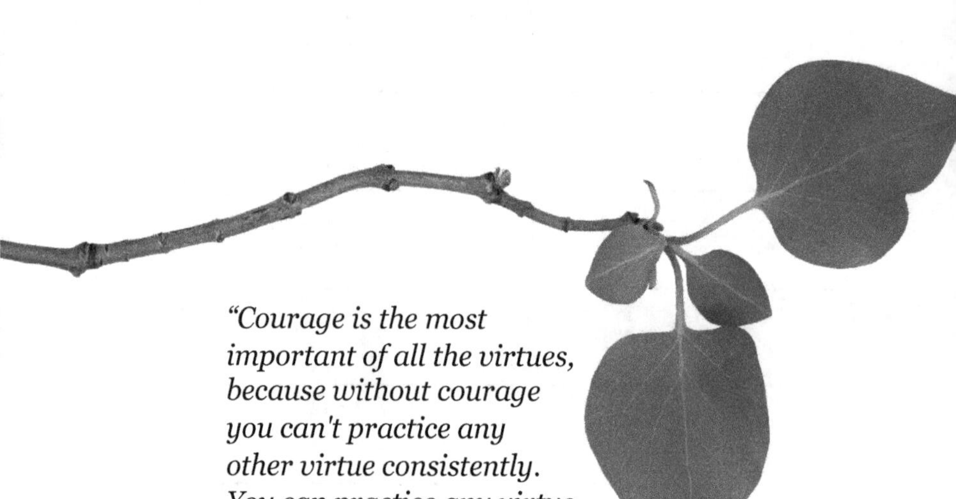

"Courage is the most important of all the virtues, because without courage you can't practice any other virtue consistently. You can practice any virtue erratically, but nothing consistently without courage."

~Maya Angelou

CHAPTER NINE

Get Your S.H.I.F.T. Together
Repetition Wins Games

I'm always going to try. My mother's words always ignite something in me. I will not stop until I have done what I said I wanted to do, sometimes to my detriment. My ex-husband would say, I had a one-track mind, and once I focused nothing else mattered. I can see where that can be difficult to accept for those in your circle who need or desire your attention, but I was driven. I was committed to achieving my goals. I knew my practice had to produce results in the form of profits.

In the past, I would often get tunnel vision and my goal became the finish line. It's that point where I would forget everything that was going on around me other than the necessary steps to accomplish the mission. Practicing patience and being able to meditate on what I deserve. I stopped worrying about what people had to say. I've always believed that if I worked hard at something, then I would be able to get it done. That attitude helped me accomplish things that once seemed impossible. But the phrase, All things are possible continued to resonate in my mind.

Game time.

I don't feel like I can be fearful about what I'm supposed to be doing. If I don't take the chance, how am I going to know? So, I guess there may be a little anxiety around it, but planning and preparation can help eliminate that anxiety. Since I was a kid, preparation was important because I always needed to do well, and I learned early that preparation was the secret. I was never the person that had to study, I could read something and retain it. When I was in school, I was always two or three levels ahead of my peers. But I was not challenged when it came to reading for comprehension, but test-taking was a different story. I didn't spend a lot of time studying to complete my coursework, which I passed with A's and B's. But to pass the exam that would allow me to graduate with my Masters, I had to take a different approach. I knew that I was not a great test taker with the type of test that I was going to be taking. So I spent months researching and preparing to take that test.

The test for this advanced degree is not a test of knowledge. This is a test, to determine if you know how to take the test, which historically Black people fail more often than not. So, I figured out all the things I needed to do to not only be acquainted with this test but also ace it. I spent a couple of months studying for it. I stayed up late and woke up early to ensure my success and it paid off. I passed the test on my first try and graduated.

The test was the obstacle in my path. I had to figure out how to either get over, around it, or find the most favorable route through it. I chose to prepare for the possibility and went through it. The preparation was a lot of work. I surveyed the landscape and decided on a course of action that best suited me. I knew myself, which means I knew my strengths and my weaknesses. I found a great resource book that became my main study tool. I studied and read, read and studied every day for months. The week before the test, I took off work for a whole week to study every day. I was confident in my knowledge; I had the information superhighway at my fingertips at all times. I could go online and pretty much find anything, ask all sorts of questions, and get insight that was not available when I was pursuing my undergraduate degree. I knew a couple of people that had taken the test, so I asked questions. I got two or three different types of testing tools to practice. I was committed to succeeding but realized I had to play differently to get favorable results. Sometimes people

don't know what to do or which resource is right for them. This usually happens because they haven't taken the time to know themselves. I knew where my power resided. I knew my strengths and my weaknesses. On test day, I got up early that morning and went to play the game I had prepared for.

Keeping your eyes focused on the finish line instead of the turmoil around you can prove beyond difficult for most. As my siblings battled drug addiction, I had to stay focused on school and graduating. I learned lessons by default, some of which I had to flip or reverse to see the positive situation during the mess. I watched my brother ride the rollercoaster of addiction for years. What I realized is that he would always relax when he had idle time and got around the old familiar faces that helped him fall victim to drugs. On the contrary, I needed to find the ideal people to surround myself with. These are the people that encourage, inspire and uplift people. If you haven't put yourself around the right people at the right places and doing the right things, you could end up making one wrong turn.

I've had many sleepless nights and days of constant work. When I started the group home for teen moms, my business partner and I began practicing fasting. We were looking for energy and wanted to reconnect with our higher power for guidance. Every time something would come up, we'd fast. While fasting we would get so much clarity. It helped me make better decisions and helped me focus my thoughts. It was all a part of the process.

I've always focused on what I could control. I believe that came from years of counseling and therapy. When I got in tune, things just kind of happened as they were supposed to happen, but I was taking control of what I was able to manage.

But managing people and processes can have its challenges. You deal with faulty processes and sometimes faulty people. Some people play the victim while others take responsibility for their actions. I recently had an incident with one of my staff members. She kept threatening to quit. She sent me this long email about some things that she felt were happening that seemed to come from nowhere and had no merit, but I chose to investigate. Upon further review and working with her for several months I quickly saw that she had some things going on in her life. So, she's one of those people who, regardless of what I say or do, it still would never be enough. I had to receive that. But she also was a good worker, so I was trying to figure out a way to work with her. In the last message that she sent, she claimed that she had some items and some other snacks that went missing from the break room refrigerator.

I had to pull my policy. I have a lost and damaged property policy. I'm not playing that game. C. Addison was not responsible for anything you brought to the facility. I had to have these policies in place because, someone could call me every day saying, "Oh, I had a soda in the refrigerator and now it's gone." Now we must write up reports.

I'm not going to call around the staff to see who's going to confess to the items. I'm running a business, not a daycare service. Time is money and that is not what we get paid to do. All employees had signed this form and understood and agreed to what I was saying at the time.

"I don't know what you want me to do, Ms. Smith," I said in a polite tone.

She proceeded to tell me she should quit. My question to her was, "Are you quitting?" She continued her threats to leave. So I say, "Are you quitting?"

"Well, I guess I'll have no choice."

"Ok, a supervisor will be there in ten minutes to relieve you." And that was that.

But that's a victim mentality that a lot of people possess. They begin to spend their whole lives in a never-ending cycle. Because you can only wear the mask, for so long...six months max then you must move on when exposed.

Many people don't take control of their lives. This begins with a willingness to look at the darkness which is what empowers you to change. For a long time, I was reluctant to address some of those things that I had experienced in my life. But even though I knew that by dealing with these things I would potentially feel better, I needed support. I also needed to work with other people who overcame similar circumstances. Dealing with these things made me feel better. You do move through it. I had built a huge wall compiled of all my experiences.

These experiences were keeping me from being who I was. I was also worried about what other people had to say about it. I had to let all of that stuff go. I had to let go of what other people thought about me. Sometimes we are stuck there because we've made a commitment and don't know how to S.H.I.F.T.

Committed to mediocracy.

When I see somebody that has a gift or some talent, I feel it in my spirit, whether they're paying me or not. I will not allow them to simply talk about doing something without doing anything about it. We're not going to keep talking about it, we're going to do something about it. I'm going to offer you resources or some advice. After that, it's up to you to take that advice or not. I'm always positive, even when I'm starting conversations with the people that I'm working with, I say, "Tell me something good about today or this week." Usually, people want to start complaining about whatever they can as soon as they can.

Until a few years ago, I would get intimidated easily. I was placed in rooms with CEOs, top executives, policymakers, and owners and was unsure if I belonged or if I was ready. One day I realized that I was invited into those rooms for a reason. I didn't understand the power of who I was, what I could accomplish, and what I had to offer the world. We all have "it" inside of us, we just have to tap into it. I write my goals down when they come. I probably have my goals written down four or five different times in different places.

You have to ask yourself the question, "What are the things that I need to work on?" And you have to be willing to do just that.

Just plant the seeds.

Different people need different things at different periods in their lives. I think some of it is a little bit of denial and some of it is just not even understanding. So, when you were planting those seeds, there was no immediate reward. The long term is, if I do these things, this is what the outcome could potentially be. So going through that process, I know I'm working towards something at the end of it.

I was not practicing the plan, because I had not connected with it. I didn't know where to start, so my logic was, I'm not going to start. To be motivated to apply this you must be able to see the possible results.

S.H.I.F.T. TIP:

No matter how tough it gets, keep going. The winners are the ones who won't stop.

SHIFT NOTES

"To my mind we should all be too busy for petty things, too big for smallness, to intelligent not to see what happens, when we stop to them."

~Ethel Hedgeman Lyle

CONCLUSION

Finish Your S.H.I.F.T.

Everything happens for a reason. I do not believe in accidents. This road that I've traveled, the steps I've applied, and the choices that I made were lessons that I needed to learn to be where I am today. This journey has prepared me for what's next, just like your journey has for you. Recently during my morning reflections, I thought about all the things, situations, and people who added value to my life along the way. Some of the things I encountered were meant to harm me, but they helped me. Some of my most challenging times birthed beautiful moments and opportunities. Taking my siblings to

Alcoholics Anonymous meetings provided an unexpected foundation for processing my feelings and working through situations. The steps they were learning that would help them beat the addiction were some of the same principles and steps I used to beat the odds and succeed.

I've been around therapy my entire life. I heard the stories and had not even realized it, but I vowed not to let it be my story. Getting those tools unconsciously, I was learning and going through treatment and probably not even realizing that I was in treatment right along with them. I was helping them, but also driving myself towards the things that would benefit my life.

For me , "Hope is being able to see there is light past the darkness." Clarindria

I knew that I was on a journey and all these things I encountered were a part of that process. If I would have done anything differently, I wouldn't be where I am now. The same goes for you. Now you may be thinking you wanted your life to turn out different. The thing is, your life doesn't just "turn out" different, but you have to make it different. You must define what you want and make that your reality.

I often remind the people that I'm around regularly that, It's enough for everybody. This means, there's a way for everybody to move in a situation to become successful. We'll never all be at the same place at the same time. We all need to be working on and towards something that inspires us to keep growing. No one wants to be around people who aren't growing. The saying says, "Show me the five people you hang around most and I'll show you your future."

We must be selective of those we choose to spend our time with.

For me, this journey was about getting in tune with who I was, to become my best self. When I was in my "coma", I merely gilded through my days on autopilot. Nothing was processed or thought through.

Now in my new life, I have released those things that no longer benefit me. I had to continue to move forward and let go of things that were out of my control. I had to work through the process and be in tune to remember that things were supposed to happen at a particular time. All things take time, by putting yourself in a position to start the work, you are setting yourself up to prosper. We all get stuck from time to time and getting started can be difficult. To circumvent the challenges, put yourself in a position to start the work, acknowledging that the work must get done for anything else to work.

My mother was independent, resourceful, forgiving to a fault at times. She explained things to me in a way that made the lesson more of a moment. She wasn't teaching, she was sharing and preparing me for the future. Heavy is the head that wears the crown I believe is how the saying goes. My mother had positioned me as the go-to, so my shoulders needed to be strong and erect to carry the load that became my life. She showed me the importance of giving myself grace, but not letting me off the hook. I can't beat myself up, but I also need to remember that there is no room for excuses. You either do it or not. It's kind of like being a little pregnant. It's just not possible. All in or nothing.

I love you. Thank you.
Please forgive me. I'm sorry.

That grace my mother reminded me to give myself was often overlooked by me. For so long I was holding on to things that no longer benefited the new Clarindria. Let go...forgive yourself for not doing it sooner but celebrate the fact that you have done it now. I don't necessarily know if I was strong enough before, but I feel I am now.

My mother's leadership made me understand that I was capable of doing something more. Whatever that looked like, it was a reminder that I could reach unimaginable heights if I just applied myself.

By incorporating a shift in your thinking, which now serves as your introduction to *Entrepreneurial Therapy*. If you surrender to the wind, you can run with it at your back, using it to propel you.

Do you remember when you let go? Or maybe you haven't let go yet. You could be holding on to toxic things that poison your mindset and often paralyze your progress.

A weight was lifted when I realized two important things:

1. I can't save everyone, and everyone is not meant to go on my journey.

2. I'm not able to control everything, life is happening in its own time.

I can continue to navigate and pray for favorable conditions, or I can quit. Quitting was never an option for me. The old version of myself worried constantly about how she was perceived and being accepted. I present confidence, so most have a hard time believing that side of me. But I do the job that is required and keep my eyes on the prize. It's a misconception that just because you exude confidence, life doesn't still happen daily. You still face obstacles and set backs, but they simply set you back rather than stopping you.

Allow me to reintroduce myself.

I came to the resolve that you either like me or you don't. I'm not going to attempt to convince you because either way, I will be ok. Those who knew me years ago would recognize the change immediately. The confidence I possess by knowing myself and being ok with who I am is enough to push me ahead by itself.

The biggest adventure you can ever take is to live the life of your dreams. I feel like I'm living that life, but I have more dreams. Although I am doing exactly what I want to do, I know there's more. I'm doing exactly what I want to do, how I want to do it and I'm not answering to anybody, but I know there's more. I know independence looks attractive and you may be searching to find your independence, but it's more than a look. Independence means you're doing the work, overcoming the setbacks, and persevering in the face of adversity. No one or any situation is perfect, every situation has its set of issues or challenges. It's your responsibility to address and deal with the set of circumstances that you've been given. The question you have to ask yourself is, how are you going to treat and take care of and nurture them? There's always going to be some things that are happening around you. It's up to you to receive that and take this stuff in or you figure things out for yourself and know what you're working on, know what you're trying to get to, because there will always be something attempting to block your path and naysayers that don't believe you can navigate past the challenges. Prove them wrong but most importantly prove yourself worthy.

Sometimes people get stuck and stop making the choices that lead to prosperity. We often make choices for the moment and neglect to consider the long-term ramifications. My story could have played out very differently. I don't shy away from that or pretend that I don't know it. I came from situations and circumstances that caused most to succumb to a list of things that seek young black women out like a disease.

From teenage pregnancy to drugs and even senseless violence. I eluded them all like the plague. I made choices that led me away from the BS, and instead, I embraced S.H.I.F.T. and made a way out of no way. I decided not to overindulge in alcohol because I knew we had that addictive gene in my family. I also chose to pursue my passion and walk in my purpose.

You've got to give up the shit that weighs you down. For me, it was my marriage. He was the number one light dimmer. No matter what I did, it wasn't right or didn't matter. When I finally accepted that he was not going to change I knew I had to get my S.H.I.F.T. and go. It was a rebirthing process. I stopped trying to get him to see my light and let it shine regardless of who saw it. Although I wanted him to be supportive of me. I wanted us to be on the same team. The reality was different, but coming out of my coma I began to not only see we were on separate teams, but we also weren't in the same league. I thought marriage meant my husband was supposed to be my biggest cheerleader.

Phylicia Rashad said, “I am just myself, and who I am is a lot.” I often laugh because I know who I am, and everyone is not ready for that. It wasn’t until after the divorce that he went to therapy and was able to acknowledge that I was a whole lotta woman that he was not prepared for, but his pride would not allow him to let me go. He was always a great father, he just wasn’t a great husband. We have been able to build a great co-parenting relationship and raise three amazing children.

Knowing that there is something bigger than me is what gets me through each day. Alone, I am not capable of doing all the things that I've done. The strength and the power have come from me believing. I know that Someone is guiding my steps. Sometimes you've got to let everything go. So if you are unhappy with anything, whatever is bringing you down, get rid of it because you'll find that when you're free, your true self emerges.

I heard Jada Pinkett Smith say, “Being in love is willing to be devastated.” I’m in love with life and pursuing my purpose. Life continues to provide moments of devastation that I've learned to push through. This brings us to this moment and this book.

The Dream.

Every great dream begins with a dreamer. You must always remember that you have within you the strength, the patience, and the passion to reach the stars and change the world. Wisdom has taught me that I begin to make that change by starting with the immediate world around me. I want to leave a legacy. I want it to be evident that I was here. I want you to make your mark, so I'm sharing the blueprint I wish I had. I've been able to blaze a trail for some to follow that are interested in my model. I have been able to help women around the world who are facing similar decisions. Women need a process to stay on course to achieve their goals despite setbacks or challenges that make the journey seemingly unbearable.

I wasn't always able to hop on a flight and go anywhere I wanted. This is 20 years in the making.

Have you thought about what it is that you're making? Will it afford you the life you dream of? I've experienced pain that I didn't think I would be able to overcome. Losing my mother was one of the hardest things I've experienced. Being molested and raped before puberty changed my view of the world and forced me to put a guard up to protect myself. But starting my business and building it to the point that I could hire my siblings gave me confidence and a sense of security. My experiences, as are yours, are the foundation of who we are and what motivates us to succeed -- or not. My experiences planted something in me that's hard to describe, but when you see it, the growth is evident.

We all have things that we must deal with. The trauma we've experienced is real and must be addressed. The myth that Blacks don't do therapy must stop being perpetuated. Therapy just might save your life. You must put your guard down and be vulnerable enough to receive the help you need to tap into your greatness. You must channel each experience. Take the hurt and use it to fuel your progression. That's the secret. Only you know what you are willing to do to make it work, change yourself or your situation. If I don't follow the steps to S.H.I.F.T., nothing happens; nothing changes. Life becomes a series of "what ifs". Understand that you cannot control the results of your actions, but you can influence them. I can't control how someone reacts to what I say, but I can control my words. Just as I cannot guarantee you will succeed because of the words on these pages, but I can guarantee that it starts with a S.H.I.F.T.!

You do not need to be a visionary to succeed, but you must have a vision. You must be able to see the finish line in the distance. You need to be able to see beyond what's in front of you. You are the dreamer in your story. It's time to visualize your S.H.I.F.T. and watch the manifestation of your dreams in real life.

"My mission in life is not merely to survive, but to thrive; and to do so with some passion, some compassion, some humor, and some style."

~Maya Angelou

SHIFT NOTES

"Just when the caterpillar thought the world was over, she became a butterfly."

~Unknown

WHO SUPPORTS YOU?

Your support system is a network of people you trust and look to for guidance. Our immediate support networks often include our family and friends for help. Support builds us up and often gives us the strength to keep going or even thrive. But support is certainly not a one-way street. For me, it was my mother who passed in 2000, I was her baby girl/bestie, and she was my biggest supporter. Her support was critical to who I became as a person and as a professional. I remember feeling less anxious because I had someone to listen to me with who I could always be honest. Getting guidance from a trusted friend, mentor, or loved one becomes more valuable than gold or diamonds. Sometimes it's just about talking things out, which I did with my mother often. Once you identify the main supporters in your life, do your best to build those relationships. Connect with them regularly and keep them updated about your life. Invite them into your decisions and explain your reasoning—then ask for their honest opinion.

You'll face both big and small challenges throughout your journey; it's important to have people to lean on in times of need. When obstacles arise, you'll need help keeping your goals in perspective. The people who support you will be there for you when you need to talk after a long day, or when you're feeling overwhelmed. Find people who will celebrate your successes and encourage you to learn from your failures and to meet each challenge with a S.H.I.F.T.ed perspective.

A message to my biggest supporter.

It's been more than 21 years since my mother passed. It has gotten a little easier over the years, but it's a lot. I continue this journey in her honor, busting down doors and making her proud. Get motivated about building a circle of support to help you stay engaged and motivated to succeed on your journey.

My mother and I would often write letters to each other. Before she passed I thought it was only right that I write her a final letter. Before she passed she asked me to include the letter in her obituary.

To Mama,

I remember when I was just a child and had no idea what life would bring, but I knew I had my mama, my mama was always there for me and down from me for whatever you know I ask myself what would I do without my mother she was my best friend the one I laughed with and cried with what do you do without your mother the one who listened always and welcomes you with open arms and believes in you when you don't believe in yourself mama that's right warm Carmel skin salt and pepper hair petite but got it going on mama my mom that's right the best mother in the whole world taught me about working to get what I want and being independent able to stand on my own if need be she taught me to not depend on a man or your best friend because they may stand you up but not my mom where is she at 2:00 a.m. waiting on the other line so you can say you made it waiting to see your new outfit you got to go out with your girl. I love you mama for eavesdropping on the phone and telling my business what little I have and telling me no sometimes and slapping the you know what out of me that's my mama I Would go On but what more can you say about a strong black woman that carried me for 9 months eating sweet potato pie and hoping I was a boy and loving me for me giving what she didn't have and always making ends meet I know it sounds like some of your mother's but there is no mistaking the one and only my mother the best mother in the whole world.

Love you
Clarindria

S.H.I.F.T. TIP

Remember to cherish those who support you, nurture the relationships and use your gift as the wind that helps you soar above the obstacles. You were created to move, why not make your next one a S.H.I.F.T.

SHIFT NOTES

CPSIA information can be obtained
at www.ICGtesting.com
Printed in the USA
BVHW041610231121
622346BV00017B/835